Original title:
The Woodland Whimsy

Copyright © 2025 Creative Arts Management OÜ
All rights reserved.

Author: Arabella Whitmore
ISBN HARDBACK: 978-1-80567-168-8
ISBN PAPERBACK: 978-1-80567-467-2

Majestic Whispers of Olde

In shadows deep where rabbits play,
A squirrel dances, hip-hip-hooray!
With acorns flying through the air,
Who knew nature had such flare?

A raccoon sings a silly tune,
Beneath the light of a chuckling moon.
The owls exchange their mock debate,
While deer join in at half-past late.

Trill and Twirl Through the Thicket

A bear in boots, how bizarre indeed,
Twirls with glee among the weed.
The fox throws confetti, what a sight,
As frogs join in with leaps of delight.

The trees, they chuckle, branches sway,
While hedgehogs roll in a spiny ballet.
Jays drop jokes from boughs so high,
As butterflies giggle and flutter by.

Glade of Glittering Dreams

In a patch of sun, the chameleons prance,
With colors bright, they love to dance.
The mushrooms wear hats, so chic and round,
While gnomes stir laughter out of the ground.

A picnic spread, the ants try to steal,
But the raccoon's plotting a sneaky meal.
The stars above twinkle their cheer,
For every creature gathers here.

Frolics in Fern Fringes

Under fern fronds, the chipmunks race,
With tiny hats, they quicken their pace.
A hedgehog critiques the dance of a hare,
While crickets chirp, declaring it fair.

A party in shadows, where mischief runs hot,
The racquets of sticks for a game they have got.
The laughter rings out, a whimsical tune,
As they dance in the light of a winking moon.

Fables of the Fern Fronds

The fronds were dancing, quite a sight,
A frog in boots, oh what a fright!
He slipped and slid, his jump went wrong,
The ferns all giggled, what a song!

A snail in glasses, smart and slow,
He read the leaves, all in a row.
"Why rush when things are going well?"
The toads all winked, a funny spell!

A wise old owl, perched up high,
Said, "Why not laugh? Just give it a try!"
The critters nodded, their hearts so light,
In this silly wood, all felt just right!

With every giggle, the forest grew,
A place where fun and fables flew.
A tale of joy, so spritely spun,
In the realm of ferns, a fabled fun!

Embrace of the Eldest Elm

There stood a tree both grand and wide,
Its branches stretched like arms, with pride.
A squirrel spun tales, cheeky and bold,
Of acorns buried, treasures untold!

The rabbits all chuckled, hopping near,
"Is it just me or did that nut appear?"
They searched and squeaked, with frantic zest,
For hidden gems, a woodland quest!

A spider spoke, with a grin so bright,
"Come dance with me in the pale moonlight!"
The bugs all twirled, in a jovial trance,
The elm just sighed, "Let's give it a chance!"

With laughter ringing, the night was long,
In the nest of arms, they sang their song.
The eldest elm, a heart so warm,
Embraced their silliness, in perfect charm!

Delight in the Dew-Dappled Dawn

At dawn's first light, the dew drops gleamed,
A ladybug winked, she seemed to beam.
"It's a great day to be tiny and bold!"
The grasshoppers chirped, "Let's break the mold!"

A bumblebee stung with a dance so sweet,
Buzzing with joy, skipping on fleet.
"Join me, dear friends, let's create some cheer!"
The flowers nodded, "We're glad you're here!"

A chorus of frogs croaked a tune,
While butterflies flitted, under the moon.
"All this delight, it makes us grin,
In the dew-dappled dawn, the fun begins!"

With every giggle and playful leap,
They wove through the woods, their joy to keep.
In the morning light, laughter was found,
A whimsical world, where silliness crowned!

Beneath Boughs of Timeless Tales

Silly squirrels dance on tree tops,
While grinning owls pretend to snooze.
The acorns roll in haphazard hops,
As woodpeckers sing their funny blues.

Beneath the branches' play-filled shade,
A rabbit juggles carrots with a cheer.
The echoes of laughter never fade,
As mushrooms giggle, spreading good cheer.

Glimmers of Stardust Among the Pines

Fireflies use glow sticks for their fights,
While chipmunks wear hats too big for their heads.
The moon chuckles softly at the sights,
As frogs recite poems from their tiny beds.

Pine cones tumble, rolling with glee,
The wind tickles leaves, making them giggle.
A deer prances, wild and free,
While crickets perform in evening's wiggle.

Journey Through the Jewelled Grove

In paths where daisies wear bright crowns,
A hedgehog rolls down a mossy hill.
With every tumble, laughter abounds,
As butterflies spin with joyful thrill.

The brook babbles tales of mud-stained shoes,
And rabbits race past with silly frights.
Every twist reveals amusing clues,
As the sun sets to bring on giggling nights.

Whimsy of Wandering Creatures

A fox in socks waltzes on by,
With raccoons selling treasures at stalls.
Each whispering breeze makes them cry,
As they tumble and bumble, having a ball.

Badgers burst into spontaneous song,
While finches gossip and chatter away.
In this kingdom, where mischief belongs,
Every day is just another play.

Enchanted Glades and Hidden Trails

In glades where squirrels dance and prance,
   A rabbit wearing shoes takes a chance.
With mushrooms sprouting hats so tall,
   And giggles echoing through it all.

A fox caught napping, snorts with glee,
While owl debates the best type of tea.
   The brook sings a tune, oh so spry,
As bees wear sunglasses, buzzing on by.

Secrets of the Sylvan Grove

In shadows deep, where secrets hum,
A hedgehog plays the bongo drum.
With acorns dropping like confetti,
A turtle claims he's quite the ready.

The trees tell tales of quirky bugs,
As rabbits play a game of hugs.
The mushrooms giggle, swaying low,
And fairies toss their leaf confetti show.

Beneath Canopy Dreams

Under skies where dreams take flight,
A snail runs races, what a sight!
With ladybugs in beauty contests,
And ants debating who is the best.

Beneath tall oaks, a party's flair,
With drumming frogs and a croaking pair.
The grass is lush, the laughter loud,
As critters gather, oh so proud.

Fables of the Fern-Flecked Forest

Among the ferns, a tale unfolds,
Of gnomes who barter glittering golds.
A bear in pajamas sings a tune,
While mice dance wildly beneath the moon.

Squirrels swap nuts for silly hats,
And owls share puns with jovial chats.
The forest bursts with whimsy bright,
A carnival of joy, pure delight.

Pixie Dust and Pine Cones

In a glen where fairies play,
Pine cones join the dance today.
Sprinkled dust that makes you grin,
Jumping squirrels, let the fun begin!

Laughter echoes through the trees,
A giggling breeze stirs up with ease.
Mushrooms wiggle, topsy-turvy,
While hedgehogs roll, looking nervy!

A fairy sneezes, oh what a sight,
Spilling sparkles, pure delight.
Bouncing rabbits in a spin,
Chasing laughter, let's dive in!

The Hidden Path of Sunlight

Where sunbeams dance on mossy ground,
Doodles of shadows twist around.
A snail declares, 'I'm in no rush,'
While chipmunks laugh, they giggle and hush.

Each flower yawns, it's time to wake,
Bees in tune, for goodness' sake!
A path of laughter, hidden from view,
With squeaky shoes and skies so blue.

The crunch of leaves, a playful sound,
With every step, new joy is found.
Silly squirrels play hopscotch here,
With acorns flying, full of cheer!

Starlit Stories Under the Oak

Underneath the old oak's shade,
Moonlight spills, a playful cascade.
Whispers of owls tell tales tonight,
As fireflies twinkle, oh what a sight!

A raccoon's caper, such funny flair,
Swapping stories without a care.
"Believe it or not," the fox will say,
"I once chased my tail all night and day!"

With crickets chirping in joyful tune,
The night spins magic under the moon.
Gathered friends, both furry and feathered,
In starry laughter, all are tethered.

Dancing Shadows on the Forest Floor

Shadows twist in a playful race,
Sunlight winks; it's a silly place.
Bugs with hats, they do a jig,
Mice in shoes, perform a gig!

The leafy curtains sway and sway,
As giggling roots join in the play.
Frogs leap high, crooning a song,
"Who's the best?" they all sing along!

Rustling branches join the cheer,
As laughter rings loud and clear.
With dancing leaves and fluttering wings,
The forest giggles, oh what joy it brings!

Magic in the Mossy Hollow

In a nook where mushrooms grin,
Squirrels dance with tiny kin.
A hedgehog rolls in leafy cheer,
While owls hoot jokes for all to hear.

Frogs jump high, then slip and slide,
Chasing sandcastles built with pride.
Fireflies flicker, lighting the stage,
Creating laughter, turning a page.

Patchwork of Petals and Pine

Bees wear hats that make them spin,
While flowers giggle, they're in a din.
The pine trees throw a party loud,
As acorns dance, they're quite proud.

A butterfly with polka dots,
Gives every bee a twisty plot.
With petals fluffed like feathery hats,
The whole grove joins in, chatting with bats.

Whirling Leaves and Whispered Dreams

Leaves twirl down in a merry flight,
As giggles echo, shy and bright.
A dancing twig begins to prance,
Making every critter take a chance.

Old pine cones gossip, lost in time,
While rabbits hop with perfect rhyme.
In every rustle, giggles seep,
Nature's humor, a secret to keep.

Journey Through a Twilight Canopy

Under stars that blink and sway,
Foxes plot a funny play.
Mice in tuxedos rush about,
Squeaking jokes with joyous shout.

The path is lit by glowing stones,
As frogs launch into silly tones.
With shadows dancing in a line,
The night's a stage for frolics fine.

Festive Frogs in the Fountain

Frogs in bow ties leap and prance,
With splashes that make the flowers dance.
They croak a tune, so bold and bright,
While dragonflies join in sheer delight.

Lily pads hold their evening feast,
With crickets playing the role of the beast.
A turtle DJ spins records right,
As the moon rises, they party all night.

One fat frog tries to take the lead,
He slips and slides—oh, what a breed!
The others laugh, they can't pretend,
In the fountain fun, there's no end.

The stars above twinkle and glow,
As frogs throw hats in a brilliant show.
With leaps and bounds, their joy does soar,
In the froggy rave, who could ask for more?

Radiant Rhapsody Among the Roots

Under trees, the squirrels play,
Chasing shadows, dancing away.
They stumble and trip on tiny seeds,
In a nutty world, fulfilling their needs.

A raccoon juggles acorns in glee,
While the birds watch from a high, leafy tree.
Their chirps form a merry old song,
As the woodland revelers gather along.

One squirrel claims he's the best of all,
In his overalls, standing proud and tall.
But a misstep sends him into a pile,
And laughter erupts—oh, what a style!

In laughter and joy, the woods come alive,
Where silly antics and songs thrive.
With roots all around, they share their cheer,
As their humble stage fills the atmosphere.

Chirping Chronicles of the Clearing

In the clearing, a cricket raps,
While his friends listen, all in laps.
They giggle at puns, so offbeat,
While the rabbits tap their tiny feet.

A hedgehog blends beats with a drum,
While owls hoot their routine hum.
Squirrels provide the background dance,
In the woodland rave, they take a chance.

One little dude wears a tiny hat,
Claims he's the coolest, but look at that!
He spins and wobbles, takes a wrong turn,
And lands with a thud—a lesson to learn!

Through the chirps and laughs, the night does fade,
While the stars above join the parade.
In the clearing's nook, where joy collides,
The woodland chronicles reel with pride.

Where Woodlands Whisper Secrets

In the hush, secrets softly pass,
From one cheeky squirrel to a blade of grass.
"Did you hear? The owls are trying to sing!"
Giggles ripple through, as the treetops swing.

A fox tells tales about the moon's last prank,
How it spilled cheese over the happy bank.
The laughter erupts, bouncing off trees,
As the breeze carries giggles with ease.

The badger joins with a joke so sly,
"Did you see that frog say goodbye?"
With snickers and chuckles echoing wide,
In the heart of the woods, no secrets hide.

As dusk falls, the whispers grow bold,
With tales of antics that never get old.
In the woodlands where laughter resides,
Secrets tumble, while joy abides.

Song of the Silver Birch

In a dress of green and white,
A tree spins round in pure delight.
With leaves that dance in a gale,
It tells jokes to a lurking snail.

A squirrel laughs, its cheeks so round,
In acorn hats, they dance around.
They stage a show on twisted roots,
Playing tricks in wobbly boots.

The silver bark, it grins so wide,
As playful winds become their guide.
The branches sway, not one, but two,
The audience—a stunned raccoon!

So if you chance upon this sight,
Take a step back, it's pure delight.
For nature plays her merry tune,
And all join in—both leaf and loon.

Tales of Tangles and Twists

Among the ferns, a secret lies,
Of knotted vines and spider spies.
The hedgehog rolls in tangled grass,
Telling all the world, "Let's pass!"

A rabbit hops with floppy ears,
While tangled webs bring out the cheers.
"Let's play hide and seek," they shout,
Yet end up lost and filled with doubt.

The grass blades serve as sneaky screens,
With tiny critters in their scenes.
They tumble over roots and stones,
Creating laughter, silly tones.

So gather 'round the leafy maze,
And join this merry game of praise.
For every twist brings giggles bright,
In nature's fun-filled, joyful light.

Twilight Sprinkles in the Pine

As dusk arrives, the tree tops gleam,
With tiny stars that glimmer, beam.
The owls wear glasses made of glass,
In search of snacks as squirrels pass.

A pinecone juggles, quite the sight,
While crickets chirp with pure delight.
The fireflies put on their best show,
In winking dances all aglow.

A raccoon tries to find a muse,
But slips and lands on muddy shoes.
The twilight giggles, soft and sweet,
As woodland critters take a seat.

When shadows stretch and night grows deep,
They tell their tales before they sleep.
And all the forest sings in tune,
To welcome in the silver moon.

Squirrels' Soiree at Sunset

Dressed in fluff and tiny hats,
The squirrels throw a party—fancy rats!
With acorn cakes and leafy drinks,
They gossip, giggle, and share winks.

Twilight cloaks the world in gold,
As silly stories start to unfold.
One claims to have flown like a bird,
But everyone knows that's quite absurd!

They dance on branches, tails held high,
As butterflies flutter, zooming by.
With every flip and every twist,
This gathering just can't be missed!

As stars come out, the night's still young,
With laughter shared and songs still sung.
The woodland's alive with cheerful sounds,
In this merry home, joy abounds.

Basking in the Fables of the Forest

In shadows where the squirrels play,
A rabbit wears a hat all day.
The raccoons dance with pots and pans,
While bears bake cakes with tiny hands.

The owls hoot jokes from branches high,
As butterflies in suits pass by.
A fox tells tales of grand delight,
While fireflies twinkle through the night.

Echoes of Laughter from the Pines

Beneath the pines, the giggles bloom,
With frogs in coats, they paint the room.
The porcupines like prickly jest,
Write rhymes upon their quill-styled chest.

A sneaky fox with funny shoes,
Tricks all the birds who squawk and snooze.
They tumble down in giggly heaps,
Chasing dreams beneath the sleeping leaves.

Celestial Fables of the Treetops

In treetops high, a playground waits,
Where squirrels act as circus mates.
They juggle acorns with such flair,
While mockingbirds perform midair.

The wise old owl gives out his cheer,
To bouncy bears who play up here.
They bounce and roll in joyous play,
As shooting stars join in the day.

Curious Creatures of the Underbrush

Beneath the leaves, the antics throng,
With hedgehogs singing silly songs.
A mole in glasses reads the news,
While all the crickets dance in shoes.

The snails wear ties to join the fun,
As beetles race like they have a gun.
A party sprouts beneath the ground,
Where laughter echoes all around.

Where Mossy Dreams Take Flight

Caterpillars wearing hats, oh my!
They dance with glee, not shy to try.
A mushroom band plays tunes so spry,
While fireflies wink as they float by.

Squirrels in tuxedos, tails held high,
Invite the rabbits for a pie in the sky.
With acorn cupcakes, they satisfy,
A feast so grand, they're all awry.

A dandelion queen with a crown of fluff,
Declares that every squirrel is just too tough.
But starlings laugh, oh aren't they gruff?
As shadows lengthen, the night gets rough.

In this green kingdom where laughter reigns,
Fanciful tales in soft, whispered strains.
So come join the frolic, forget the pains,
Where nonsense blooms and joy never wanes.

Beneath the Boughs of Mystery

Beneath the leafy canopies, giggles abound,
A raccoon in pajamas, quite profound.
He juggles berries, oh look at him bound,
While ants throw a party, all around.

A wise old owl wearing bright glasses,
Keeps tally of the hat-wearing masses.
With a twinkle and hoot, as time passes,
He shakes his head at their silly antics.

The ferns conspire with the dancing breeze,
Whispers of mischief behind the trees.
A hedgehog's joke causes fits of wheeze,
As laughter erupts and flows with ease.

In the corners where shadows grow,
All woodland folk find a way to show,
That life's a circus beneath the glow,
Of a moon that giggles and loves the show.

Twilight's Embrace in the Evergreens

When twilight whispers secrets untold,
The critters gather, both bold and old.
A fox plays cards, the stakes are gold,
While laughter dances in the air, uncontrolled.

Pinecone hats upon their heads,
The squirrels tell tales that spinning threads.
With gummy worms, even a worm spreads,
A banquet's setup where no one dreads.

Twirling fireflies add a glow to the scene,
As bunnies break out in a quirky routine.
They hop and they skip, so light and keen,
Creating mischief with glee so serene.

Under the stars, the fun won't cease,
As woodland creatures bask in peace.
For in this grove, hilarious release,
Lives and twinkles, a joyous fleece.

Mischief in the Meadow

In a meadow where daisies tilt and twine,
A goat on a skateboard draws a line.
Chasing butterflies with great design,
Declares that all flowers are sweet as wine.

With frogs in tuxedos playing croak,
They leap in rhythm to every joke.
A rabbit, quite clever, crafts his cloak,
And giggles arise as the daisies choke.

A sneaky snail rolls dice on the path,
Calculating fortunes, evoking a laugh.
The wind whirls around with a gentle swath,
As critters join in, their playful craft.

At dusk they declare, "We'll tear up the night!"
With starlit pranks and laughter so bright.
A merry melee, pure delight,
In this playful haven, all feels right.

Tales of the Tanglewood

In the thicket, squirrels dance,
Chasing shadows, take a chance.
Rabbits giggle in a row,
Hiding laughs where no one goes.

A raccoon wears a tiny hat,
Strutting proud, imagine that!
Frogs croak jokes on lily pads,
While the owls watch, feeling glad.

Giggling leaves in the breeze sway,
Mischief blooms in bright array.
Fireflies twinkle, limbs entwine,
Crafting tales of the divine.

In the woods, nonsense is king,
Every creature loves to sing.
With a burst of joyful cheer,
Life's a show—a laugh we share!

Chronicles of the Charms at Twilight

Under stars, the critters meet,
Badgers bustling on tiny feet.
Hedgehogs wearing shades of green,
Join the party, what a scene!

Frolicking foxes spin and twirl,
Singing songs that make you whirl.
A wise old owl hoots a rhyme,
Timing perfectly—what a crime!

Bats on swings swing low and fast,
Hopping over shadows cast.
Silly whispers fill the night,
Underneath the moon's soft light.

Every rustle brings a smile,
Joy spread thick across each mile.
In this wood, the funny reigns,
Laughter dances through the lanes!

Enchanted Grove Serenade

In the grove, the jesters play,
Chasing giggles through the day.
A hedgehog prances with a grin,
Spinning tales where fun begins.

Raccoons juggle acorns high,
While the turtles wave goodbye.
Squirrels slip on floppy hats,
Dancing wild with silly chats.

Fireflies light the merry scene,
Winking bright, a festive sheen.
Bunnies deep in playful glee,
Share their secrets, one, two, three.

In this glade, delight abounds,
With the silliest of sounds.
Nature's rhythm, sweet and clear,
Brightens every heart drawn near!

Moonlit Forest Reverie

Moonlit paths where gnomes reside,
Craft wild stories, fun to guide.
With dancing mushrooms, hats so tall,
Laughter echoes, one and all.

Mice in tuxedos take a bow,
Performing stunts, oh wow, oh wow!
Even hedgehogs sing a note,
Riding on a tiny boat.

The wise old trees sway their limbs,
Tickling clouds as humor brims.
Crickets chirp in laughter, bright,
Creating joy throughout the night.

With a wink, the forest glows,
Dancing light in funny shows.
Every nook, a giggle keeps,
In this realm where laughter leaps!

Palette of Nature's Whimsy

In the forest where squirrels play,
Colors burst, bright as the day.
A purple tree with polka dots,
Teasing napping sleepy spots.

Stripes of orange on the ground,
Giggling leaves that spin around.
A chubby mushroom wears a hat,
Wobbling as the critters chat.

A rainbow fox with silly socks,
Dances while the rabbit mocks.
With every step, the flowers sway,
In this parade of bright display.

Ticklish grass that makes you sneeze,
Bumblebees buzzing, aiming to please.
Nature's laugh is never still,
Crafting joy against our will!

Adventure Beneath the Branches

Beneath the arching leafy throne,
Where acorns gather to be grown,
A sneaky snail in shiny shell,
Wonders if he's casting spells.

A raccoon with a sticky paw,
Steals a sandwich—what a flaw!
Chasing shadows with a jibe,
While clever owls begin to vibe.

The baby deer, quite out of place,
Trips over bumbles, full of grace.
With every tumble, laughter swells,
Echoing through the woodland bells.

Under twinkling starlit shows,
Frogs leap about in silly clothes.
Adventures call and off they go,
Wobbling feet in a charming flow!

Dance of the Dainty Dandelions

In fields where dandelions sway,
They twirl and spin, a grand ballet.
A breeze whispers, they giggle light,
Inviting critters for a night.

With tiny hats made of soft mist,
King Bumblebee cannot resist.
His blurred wings in joyous hum,
Frolic in dreams, they dance and drum.

The ladybugs join the scene,
Polka-dotted, bright, and keen.
Each flap an echo, chirp and tune,
Underneath the smiling moon.

As petals flutter, laughter chimes,
Tickling toes with silly rhymes.
A festival beneath the skies,
In nature's dance, joy never dies!

Unseen Architects of the Undergrowth

A tiny beetle with a plan,
Constructs his home—a bold little man.
With twigs and leaves, he works all night,
His dreams emerging in morning light.

The ants march in their strict parade,
Building kingdoms in sun and shade.
With each grain of sand they hoard,
Their laughter's bright, never bored.

A curious owl watches wide,
As all the creatures work with pride.
With winks and nods, they share their cheer,
Inventive minds, nothing to fear.

They conjure magic, make it real,
In secret places where they feel.
Crafty hands and magic foes,
In every nook, joy freely grows!

Hummingbird Harmonies

Tiny flutters in the air,
Buzzing laughter everywhere.
Chasing shadows, bright and light,
Sipping nectar, such delight.

Colorful coats with zippy moves,
Dancing here, they've got the grooves.
A comic race, a whirl and spin,
In this joy, let the fun begin!

With beaks as tiny as a seed,
These little tricks, it's all they need.
Flapping fast, but never tired,
They play all day, they're truly wired!

Whirling through the blooms so sweet,
With every dive, they can't be beat.
Giggles sprinkle in each flight,
As they zip off into the night.

Echoes of Ancient Oak

Underneath the mighty boughs,
Whispers float, and laughter sows.
Branches twist in mischievous ways,
Telling tales of silly days.

Roots that tickle when you tread,
Branches overhead stretch and spread.
A squirrel sneezes, tries to hide,
While the acorn takes a wild ride!

Knots and grooves with secrets to share,
While the chipmunks scamper without a care.
Echoing giggles through the years,
Nature's laughter, sweet and clear.

Old oak trees bend just to peek,
At the shenanigans so unique.
Join the revelry near and far,
In this jolly woodland bazaar.

The Mischief of Mushrooms

Round and plump in their cozy beds,
They wiggle up and shake their heads.
Underneath the leafy drapes,
Fungi cheer and share their gapes.

A funny hat on top they wear,
With colors bright, beyond compare.
Dancing to the forest's tune,
In moonlight glow, beneath the moon.

They giggle low, they giggle loud,
Growing taller, feeling proud.
A caper here, a twisty prance,
Invite the critters for a dance!

In patches tangled, free and wild,
Nature hosts a playful child.
With every pop and every sprout,
Fun unfolds, there's no doubt!

Goblin Giggles in the Glade

In a glade where the green grass sways,
Goblin friends make merry plays.
With cheeky grins and tiny feet,
They share secrets, oh what a treat!

Juggling apples, bright and round,
Rolling on the soft, warm ground.
A burst of laughter fills the air,
As they tumble here, without a care.

Underneath the leafy shade,
Tiny pipsqueaks laugh and invade.
Poking noses in a game,
Seeking giggles, never shame!

They caper through the brushy leaves,
Slipping past, as nature weaves.
With each cheer and each delight,
This magical scene shines so bright.

Glimmers of Green in the Gloom

In the depths where shadows play,
Mushrooms dance in bright array.
A fox in socks, so out of place,
Chasing butterflies at a lopsided pace.

Hares wear hats that tilt and swoon,
While owls hoot a funky tune.
Leaves chuckle in a breezy jest,
As squirrels put on their acorn fest.

Beneath the ferns, a snail does race,
In a tiny car, a joyful chase.
Glimmers peek through branches tight,
The forest giggles with delight.

Toadstools tiptoe on tiny feet,
Chasing each other, what a feat!
Yet ripe ripe berries burst with cheer,
Singing songs all woodland near.

Crescendo of Crickets' Chorus

At dusk, the crickets start their show,
With violins made from reeds, they bow.
A cat in a cape joins the spree,
Dancing on the porch, so carefree.

Fireflies twinkle like stars above,
The air is sweet with a hint of love.
Grasses sway to the rhythmic song,
As everyone hums along.

Frogs in tuxedos hop to the beat,
Tap dancing on their warty feet.
All critters gather, what a sight,
In this symphonic, starry night.

With each chirp, a chuckle bursts,
Life in the thicket, it surely flirts.
Bats buzz by, in twirls and spins,
While mischief brews in the evening winds.

Pondering Paths of the Thicket

Among the trails where moonlight beams,
Wanderers ponder their silly dreams.
A raccoon, with a map quite absurd,
Looks for treasure, but just finds a bird.

Beneath a log, a frog writes a play,
About the critters who frolic and sway.
A badger dressed like a famous star,
Plays piano on a fallen tar.

The party starts when dusk unfolds,
With giggles that reach the heart's strong holds.
A lost hare shares a comic's plight,
As trees chuckle at the comic's fright.

Seeing paths with all their twists,
Each footstep marks a tale that exists.
In every turn, surprise awaits,
A burst of laughter while joy creates.

Sprites and Shadows in Sunlight

In the reservoir of sunlight's glow,
Sprites play peekaboo, oh so slow.
With painted wings, they glide and flit,
Sending shadows that dance and split.

A gnome with jests tells tales of yore,
While sprinkled flour fly from the forest floor.
With each cosmic giggle, they sparkle bright,
Creating a carnival of delight.

Dewdrops race on blades of grass,
As ants in tuxedos elegantly pass.
A bumblebee buzzes a merry tune,
Drawing flowers into a dance, a boon!

Laughing echoes through the trees,
As friends unite in a joyous breeze.
With every flutter, every glance,
Nature whispers, and the woodlands prance.

Woven Tales of the Wild

In the forest where the squirrels play,
A raccoon dances just for pay.
He juggles nuts with tiny paws,
And giggles loud at nature's laws.

Beneath the trees, the owls debate,
On why they're always staying late.
They wisecrack about their midnight flight,
While foxes act out scenes of fright.

A family of deer prances around,
With antlers up, they shake the ground.
Their secret? A dance that brings out cheer,
As rabbits join their merry deer.

Each tale spun in this lively place,
Ends with a laugh, a smirk, a grace.
In the wild's embrace, hilarity gleams,
As nature stitches together its dreams.

A Tapestry of Twilights

As twilight falls, the shadows play,
A hedgehog rolls in a comical way.
He trips on roots with a silly squeak,
While fireflies gather to take a peek.

Bats swoop low, in search of snacks,
Chasing after the giggling shacks.
They tie their capes, then zip and zoom,
Through trees that sway like giant brooms.

A wise old turtle tells a joke,
As nearby, a clumsy badger chokes.
His laughter echoes, a rippling sound,
In the whimsical realm where fun is found.

In this dusk, with all its charms,
The forest wraps us in its arms.
We chuckle and cheer, dance with delight,
In a tapestry woven of laughter bright.

Nature's Giggle Among the Ferns

Amidst the ferns, there's a cheeky breeze,
Whispering secrets to honeybees.
They buzz, they dance, in a golden swirl,
While snails plot mischief in a slow twirl.

The toadstools laugh in polka dot styles,
As bunnies hop and share their wiles.
A hedgehog's quill is a tickling tool,
He pokes at friends, the playful fool.

A parade of ants in tiny hats,
Marching proudly, those tiny brats.
They giggle and squeak about their new find,
In the leafy theatre, laughter unconfined.

From frog serenades to chirping rooks,
Nature spins tales with funny hooks.
Each rustle, each sound, a playful jest,
In the ferns, whimsy never rests.

Pastoral Interlude in the Glade

In a glade where flowers sing,
A rambling goat pretends to king.
He prances about with a crown of leaves,
As the rabbits roll and clutch their knees.

The daisies giggle; the sunbeams dance,
While a frog considers a goofy romance.
He croaks sweet nothings to butterflies bright,
Who flit and flutter, just out of sight.

A bashful sheep in a floppy hat,
Tries to hide but can't, imagine that!
The piglets snort, joining in the fun,
As they tumble over, one by one.

In this pastoral scene, such cheer abounds,
With chuckles and snorts as joy resounds.
A symphony of laughter fills the air,
In the glade, where whimsy is everywhere.

Snippets of Sunlight and Dew

In the morning, the drops play,
Dancing on leaves where the critters sway.
A squirrel in shades of brown does twirl,
Chasing a butterfly, giving a whirl.

Beneath the branches, shadows sneak,
A toe-tapping mouse, oh what a freak!
He spins and hops, what a sight to see,
As dandelions wish for a cup of tea.

Each beam of light joins in the fun,
Painting the world as if just begun.
With giggles of grass, and smiles anew,
Nature's own jesters, all in a brew.

Oh, snippets of sunshine, laughter in dew,
Playful antics of critters, askew.
In this merry glade, where joy is the cue,
Let's dance with delight, all day through!

Revelry of the Rustling Underbrush

Through the thicket, whispers flit,
Frogs in bow ties, ready to sit.
A hedgehog wears goggles, quite the sight,
As fireflies wink, lighting the night.

The bushes chime in a jolly tune,
As raccoons juggle beneath the moon.
With laughter abound and mischief galore,
Tickling branches, who could ask for more?

The laughter of leaves in a breezy spree,
Sets the stage for a grand jubilee.
Each rustle a giggle—a festive excuse,
In the theater of green, let's cut loose!

So join the parade of shrubbery joy,
Where each little critter's a playful ploy.
In the revelry bright, let's all take a plunge,
Join in the fun—come, don't make us grunge!

Mysteries of the Mirthful Maple

Oh, the maple stands with stories to tell,
Of cheeky little squirrels casting their spell.
With smug little smiles and acorns on hand,
They giggle at secrets—the best in the land.

A button-eyed owl hoots a riddle,
While watching shy rabbits dance in the middle.
Leaves dance like fluttering socks in a breeze,
As whispers of mischief flurry with ease.

With branches that wave like a jolly old friend,
This tree loves to giggle, no need to pretend.
Every knot has a story, every leaf a jest,
In the heart of the forest, it's truly the best.

So come, gather round, let the laughter unfold,
In the mysteries woven, the brave and the bold.
With joy that's contagious, join in the chase,
Under the gaze of the maple's embrace!

Gossamer Threads of Twilight

As twilight spins its silk-colored thread,
The giggles of insects fill up the spread.
A bumblebee bets with a twinkling star,
"Catch me if you can!"—it's never too far.

Fireflies flicker like cheeky old tales,
While the shadows play tag, with giggles and wails.
An owl does the cha-cha on branch up high,
And the stars hold their breath, watching the sky.

With each twirl of dusk, new antics awake,
The nightbirds serenade with no room for ache.
Every breeze carries laughter and cheer,
Tickling the cheeks of those who draw near.

So gather your wonders as daylight takes flight,
In the gossamer glow, bliss swells like a kite.
In the magic of night, let our dreams take flight,
For every laugh shared makes the stars feel bright!

Frolics of the Forest Fauna

Squirrels wearing tiny hats,
Chasing each other round the mats.
Bunnies bounce with silly glee,
While raccoons sip their iced tea.

Deer in shades of striped pajamas,
Playing cards with friendly llamas.
A fox in socks tries to dance,
But ends up tripping on his pants.

Owl's wise jokes make all of laugh,
While badgers draw up funny drafts.
The trees shake from all the fun,
As shadows play beneath the sun.

At dusk, they join a grand parade,
With silly tunes that they have made.
Each critter dons a goofy grin,
Waiting for their night to begin.

Whispers Among the Willow

Willows whisper jokes to breeze,
As ducks skate past with utmost ease.
Frogs leap in their polka dot suits,
While turtles tap dance in their boots.

A chatty crow shares funny tales,
Of sneaky mice and clever snails.
The sunbeams giggle on the stream,
As laughter floats like a sweet dream.

Fireflies spark in synchrony,
Winking like a comedy spree.
The crickets chirp a waltz so bright,
As night enchants this playful sight.

Amidst the branches, dreams take flight,
With all the critters feeling light.
They sing their tunes beneath the stars,
Their laughter echoing near and far.

Moonlit Murmurs in the Thicket

Under moonlit beams, they creep,
With critters gathering for a sweep.
A hedgehog wears a crown so proud,
While fireflies twinkle in the crowd.

A snail in glasses tells a joke,
As laughter rises like the smoke.
The raccoons join with pots and pans,
Creating beats that shake their fans.

Bats swoop low with cheeky grins,
While porcupines show off their spins.
Mice play tag in silly circles,
Startling owls with their quick hurdles.

The night is filled with giggles and squeaks,
As every creature shares their quirks.
In the thicket, magic sings,
A symphony of woodland things.

Dancing Shadows of Mossy Mounds

Mossy mounds with a wink and sway,
Invite the critters out to play.
With shadows dancing left and right,
They frolic in the soft moonlight.

Grasshoppers jump with zany style,
While turtles groove with a sly smile.
The buzzing bees lead a conga line,
As ants march by, keeping time.

A badger spins and trips on roots,
While otters wear their fashionable suits.
Laughter echoes through the trees,
As whimsy flows upon the breeze.

The night concludes with one last cheer,
As critters grin from ear to ear.
They gather close for a group hug,
Beneath the stars, their hearts are snug.

A Serenade for the Sun-Dappled

A squirrel in shades, quite a sight,
Dancing with nuts in the warm sunlight.
He trips on a root, makes a comical leap,
While giggling blooms just dance and peep.

The butterflies laugh, with colors so bold,
As they tease the ants, both daring and old.
A mischievous breeze, with a tickle and whirl,
Sends hats flying high – oh, what a twirl!

Napping beneath the great oaks so wide,
A bear dreams of berries and a picnic ride.
He wakes with a snort, in a patch of green,
Grumbling for honey, looking quite mean.

So come join the fun, leave your cares behind,
In this realm of laughter, let joy unwind.
With critters and chuckles, in sunbeams we bask,
A day in the wild, oh so many to ask!

Fairies at Dusk

As shadows grow long and the sky turns pink,
Fairies gather round, giggling – don't blink!
With wands made of daisies, and laughter like bells,
They play silly pranks, casting curious spells.

They sprinkle some glitter on a toad's head,
And watch as he jumps, startling a bed.
"Ribbit!" he hops, then he trips on a leaf,
The fairies all roar, oh, they're beyond belief!

A gnome with a hat twice his size, quite a sight,
Stumbles on mushrooms, topsy-turvy flight.
The fairies, they gather, all giggles and glee,
As petals all flutter from each laughing tree.

As twilight sets in, and stars start to shine,
The fairies, still laughing, sip dew from a vine.
In mischief they dance, under moon's soft glow,
In the heart of the forest, where joy will bestow.

Songbirds' Serenade

In the cool of the morn, the songbirds take flight,
With harmonies soaring, oh what a delight!
One trills a sweet tune, another goes 'tweet,'
In feathered attire, they shuffle their feet.

A crow joins the choir, with a caw so profound,
And the robins all giggle, all over the ground.
They swap silly notes, 'tis a kooky affair,
A duet's mishap, feathers everywhere!

A finch tells a joke, about worms in a stew,
While the doves offer wisdom – strange, but it's true!
Laughter resounds, as they peck at the seeds,
In this symphony bright, where friendship proceeds.

So let's sing along, in the morning's embrace,
With melodies swirling, full of joy and grace.
In the branches above, a party unfolds,
Where the heart sings its truth, and laughter beholds!

Swaying Secrets of the Sylva

In branches that sway, the woods start to sway,
With whispers of secrets, wild games on display.
A rabbit slips past, with a top hat askew,
He stumbles on stones, finding laughter is due.

The hedgehogs unite, with a roll and a spin,
In a race to the thicket – oh, where to begin?
With shouts of delight, and much squeaking too,
They tumble and tumble – what a marvelous crew!

A fox with a grin starts a riddle or two,
With giggles and chuckles, the woodland crew grew.
"Why did the owls take wing at the dawn?"
They hoot and they howl till the laughter is gone.

The pines sway to music that only they hear,
As critters share stories, raising a cheer.
In daylight's embrace, there's mischief galore,
In the heart of the woodland, where fun is the core!

Secrets of the Sylvan Glade

In the glade where squirrels dance,
Secret whispers take their chance.
Mushrooms wear top hats so fine,
While rabbits sip on dandelion wine.

The wise old owl starts to chuckle,
As hedgehogs form a wild huddle.
Ladybugs in polka dot shirts,
Tell tales of mischief, laughter flirts.

Frogs croon in their best opera voice,
As fireflies illuminate with poise.
Each leaf a stage for a fancy feast,
While the ants perform their marching, at least.

Balloons made of petals fill the air,
As flowers giggle without a care.
Today, the glade is filled with glee,
Secrets shared in their jubilee.

Symphony of the Woodland Creatures

A raccoon strums on a twig harp,
While crickets join in, making a lark.
Deer prance lightly in rhythmic time,
As this nature band sings in mime.

Chirpy sparrows hum their sweet tune,
With melodies that make the day bloom.
While field mice tap dance on soft grass,
In a lively show that none could surpass.

The badger drums on a hollow log,
As hedgehogs roll in the dew like a fog.
Each bush vibrates with laughter and sound,
In this playful realm, joy knows no bound.

As the sun sets in hues of delight,
Firefly dancers twinkle, taking flight.
A symphony of giggles fills the glen,
Where creatures decide to play once again.

Fluttering Fantasies Among Foliage

Beneath the leaves, a secret plot,
A fairy twirls in a blooming pot.
Gnome with a beard, so fluffy and bright,
Tries to catch butterflies in pure delight.

A butterfly pulls a prank on a mouse,
Who jumps and twirls, scared to leave the house.
While mushrooms giggle, toppled in the mud,
They talk about clouds and rain, oh what a flood!

Chasing dreams in a sunbeam's slip,
While hedgehogs plot a tiny trip.
With acorns as hats, they strut like kings,
In the land where nothing makes proper sense, it sings!

As shadows grow long and stars peek through,
Squirrels share tales of what they wish to do.
A dance unfolds amidst the trees,
Fluttering fantasies ride the breeze.

Echoes in the Enchanted Thicket

In a thicket where echoes play,
A fox tries to make a funny ballet.
The bushes laugh as he trips on a root,
While the owl hoots—what a hoot!

With vines as lassos, a raccoon tugs,
Hunting for treasure amid the shrugs.
While wily crows cackle overhead,
They plot to steal crumbs from the cake spread.

The hedgehogs run a game of charades,
With thickets ringing with jovial cascades.
Each rustle in leaves brings whimsical cheers,
As giggles float like echoes through years.

Whimsical shadows dance under the moon,
While frogs harmonize a silly tune.
Echoes of laughter fill the air,
In this enchanted world, they share.

Whispers of the Ancient Trees

Beneath the boughs where squirrels leap,
The trees will gossip, secrets deep.
They chuckle low, they creak and sway,
A riddle wrapped in rustling play.

The owls they hoot in quirks and tones,
While acorns drop like tiny bones.
A raccoon winks with mischief's flair,
His fuzzy paws dance in the air.

With branches swaying, laughter flows,
In breezy whispers, anything goes.
Unseen sprites play hide and seek,
Among the roots, so sly and sleek.

So if you wander through this glade,
Be ready for a fun parade.
For in these woods, the jokes run free,
With every rustle, pure glee you'll see.

Dances in the Dappled Light

In patches bright where shadows flit,
The critters join, they won't just sit.
A bunny twirls, a fox glides by,
They gather round, oh me, oh my!

A dancing snail with glittery shell,
Spins in circles, oh so swell.
The sunbeams laugh, they bounce around,
As flowers sway to nature's sound.

With tapping feet and flapping ears,
The woodland crew forgets their fears.
Each twist and turn, a joyful sight,
In dappled beams, oh what delight!

So join the fun, don't be quite shy,
In the merry dance, give it a try.
For here in this enchanted space,
Every step's a frolic, full of grace.

Dreaming Beneath the Canopy

Nestled soft on mossy beds,
The critters dream with sleepy heads.
A chipmunk snores, his cheeks so round,
While butterflies dance, close to the ground.

In dreamy clouds, they play and prance,
A forest ball, a nighttime dance.
The stars peek through with twinkling eyes,
As playful breezes kiss the skies.

The fireflies twinkle, a blinky show,
While crickets serenade down below.
In this realm where dreams take flight,
Each slumbering soul laughs through the night.

Awake or not, it's all the same,
In this woodland, it's a funny game.
With giggles echoing through the trees,
Dreaming softly, sweet as a breeze.

Lullabies of the Leafy Realm

When twilight falls, the leaves will sway,
In a lullaby, they softly play.
A squirrel hums, with tiny paws,
As sleepy creatures gently pause.

The brook will gurgle a soothing tune,
While fireflies dance beneath the moon.
An owl hoots, a sleepy jest,
As night takes stage, it knows the best.

A badger yawns, his dreams take flight,
In the leafy realm of pure delight.
With whispers low, the world finds peace,
In nature's arms, all troubles cease.

So close your eyes, let laughter flow,
In each soft dream where wonders grow.
With leafy lullabies in the air,
Sleep tight, my friend, without a care.

The Jester of the Jade Woods

In the forest where the trees wear smiles,
A jester trips over roots and tiles.
With a wink and a laugh, he jigs away,
Poking fun at owls who nap all day.

His hat is bright, with bells that chime,
Squirrels dance, keeping perfect time.
He juggles acorns, makes them roll,
While rabbits just can't help but stroll.

Each creature giggles at his silly game,
As the breeze carries his pun-filled name.
With every tumble, he spreads delight,
Even the shadows chuckle at night.

So if you wander through these trees,
Keep an eye out for some comic fees.
For in these woods, where laughter blends,
The jester's joy never truly ends.

Murmurs in the Meadow's Heart

In a meadow where the daisies sway,
A gossiping breeze has much to say.
It whispers secrets, tickles the grass,
While butterflies laugh as they boldly pass.

A bumblebee buzzes, it's quite the show,
Dancing to tunes only daisies know.
The frogs croak loudly, claiming their throne,
As crickets join in with a cheerful tone.

All around, nature's wisecracks abound,
Each rustling leaf, a comedic sound.
The sun pokes fun at clouds passing by,
As squirrels, in jest, leap toward the sky.

So if you pause to hear the play,
Of meadow's whispers in light-hearted sway,
You'll find the joy in every part,
For laughter blooms within the meadow's heart.

Songs of Sun and Shadows

When sunlight beckons through leafy screens,
 Shadows shimmy in their playful routines.
 Squirrels sing high, while crickets, in tune,
 Hum silly songs by the light of the moon.

A squirrel dons shades with a swaggering strut,
 While ladybugs giggle, oh what a glut!
 Frogs croak at noon, trying out their best,
 As flowers join in for a frolic fest.

The sun plays tricks, giving spots to chase,
 While shadows tumble in a wild race.
 A chuckle from owls perched high, so wise,
At the sight of lost bunnies that always surprise.

In this grand play where sun fills the air,
 Laughter erupts everywhere you dare.
 Embrace the whimsy, let your heart sing,
 For in this dance, joy is the king.

Laughter in Lily-Laden Lagoon

In a lagoon where the lilies float,
A frog rehearses with a comical coat.
Splashing tunes as he bounces about,
Each rippling wave sounds a giggling shout.

Dragonflies dart, like jesters in flight,
Tickling the toads with pure delight.
The bubbles rise up with a chuckle and cheer,
While turtles nod gently, enjoying the beer.

Laughter echoing with every splash,
Fish join in with a daring dash.
The moon grins down with a wink and a swoon,
Amidst this whimsy, chaos is a boon.

So dive in deeper, let laughter reign,
For in this lagoon, joy's never in vain.
Every lily and leaf holds a whimsical song,
Where laughter lingers, and nothing feels wrong.

Rhythm of the Rustling Leaves

Leaves chuckle and twirl, what a sight,
In the breeze, they dance with delight.
A squirrel pops up, wearing a hat,
Like a tiny magician, imagine that!

Branches sway low, like they want to play,
While the sun joins in, brightening the day.
Each gust of wind whispers a joke,
The trees laugh loud, in their leafy cloak.

A Whirl of Wildflowers

Petals twirl in a colorful spree,
Bumblebees buzz with silly glee.
"Hey there, flower!" they chant and cheer,
"Your fragrance is simply the best all year!"

Daisies compete with a wink and a smile,
"Look at me dance! I've got style!"
Buttercups giggle as they sway around,
In this vibrant circus, joy knows no bound.

Luminous Fireflies at Dusk

Little lights flicker, they zoom and dart,
Fireflies playing a glowing art.
"I'm faster!" claims one with a zestful shout,
"Catch me if you can!" then it zips out.

In the warm night, laughter fills the air,
Chasing their tails without a care.
Stars join the show, twinkling in sync,
While insects giggle and dance on the brink.

Secrets Shared by Squirrels

Squirrels gather, all chitter and chat,
"Did you see that? A cat! Imagine that!"
They exchange stories atop a tall tree,
"Who's brave enough to climb down and flee?"

With acorns stashed for a nutty delight,
They plot and they plan through day and night.
A squirrel jokes, "I'm the king of this park!"
And they all burst out laughing, bright as a spark.

Treetop Tales of Timelessness

In a tree so tall and spry,
Squirrels dance, oh my, oh my!
They wear tiny hats, quite absurd,
And gossip like the wildest bird.

Down below, the rabbits play,
Telling jokes to lighten the day.
With carrots lined up for a race,
They hop and giggle, full of grace.

A woodpecker drums a silly beat,
As raccoons prance on their tiny feet.
Each branch tells stories full of cheer,
In a world where laughter's always near.

With acorns flying, a friendly feud,
The chipmunks' antics, entirely crude!
Yet every critter knows the score,
Timeless tales from tree to floor.

Elven Echoes in the Elders' Embrace

Elves prance softly in leafy glades,
Tickling ferns, making parades.
With laughter that skips like stones,
They share secrets in hushed tones.

Underneath the ancient trees,
They serve tea brewed with honeybees.
In cups of acorn, silly dreams,
Where every sip is a burst of gleams.

Whispers ride the feathered breeze,
As elves tease the old roots with ease.
Their jigs and jests make branches sway,
Creating music, light and gay.

Echoes bounce off bark so wise,
And even mushrooms giggle and rise!
In their embrace, the world's a glee,
With every joke, a jubilee.

Sprightly Breezes and Fluttering Leaves

Breezes dance through rustling leaves,
Tickling whispers nobody believes.
The trees chuckle with a creaky laugh,
As branches wiggle in a leafy gaff.

A dandy beetle dons a tie,
While ladybugs zoom by, oh my!
With polka-dotted umbrellas in hand,
They gossip and giggle, utterly grand.

In the dappled light, shadows sway,
As playful breezes join the fray.
A grasshopper strums his tiny guitar,
Draws all the critters near and far.

With every flutter and every swirl,
The forest bursts with joy's own twirl.
A silly song on nature's breath,
In this mischief lies their depth.

The Lullaby of Lichen and Light

Once the sun slips out of sight,
Lichens sing in the dim twilight.
With voices soft like cotton fluff,
They croon of magic, sweet and tough.

Mossy rocks become a stage,
As crickets chirp with boundless rage.
The fireflies light up the night,
In a glow of giggles, pure delight.

Toadstools tap with little feet,
As shadows mingle, oh so sweet.
A waltz of whimsy in the dark,
With every note, they leave a mark.

Under the stars, where dreams take flight,
Creatures ponder life's comical plight.
In lichen's lullaby, wonder swirls,
As laughter echoes and twirls.

Streams of Serenity in the Silvan

In a glade where fairies spill,
A frog in a crown feels quite the thrill.
He croaks a tune for the dancing leaves,
While squirrels giggle, in playful eaves.

Beneath a tree, the rabbits stare,
Practicing hops with little care.
A dandelion whispers, 'Jump and twirl!'
While a mouse steps out in a tiny whirl.

The brook sings songs, a bubbly stream,
As turtles lay back, lost in a dream.
A mischief of mice shares cheese, not fright,
And the sun dips low, turning day into night.

In laughter shared, their antics freeze,
A world of whimsy in every breeze.
With every rustle, a chuckle blooms,
Nature's comedy in hidden rooms.

Heartbeats of the Hidden Haven

A chipmunk in a top hat struts with flair,
His acorn staff waving in playful air.
He challenges the birds with an impromptu race,
While the owls hoot loud, a wise old brace.

A hedgehog rolls by on a skateboard fast,
While critters cheer on, their shadows cast.
The moths throw a ball, it glows in the dark,
As the crickets join in with a chirpy lark.

In this nook, there's a dance so grand,
With fireflies leading this zesty band.
They twirl and spin in this luminous night,
With snickers erupting at every delight.

The fun never ends, it's a merry spree,
A gathering of jesters beneath the tree.
In this nook, the laughter swells,
Among hidden hearts, their joy compels.

Sprightly Spirits of the Shade

Beneath the arch where shadows play,
A squirrel wears glasses, calls it a day.
He reads a book in a wise old tone,
While wishing for chocolate, not to be alone.

A sprite with a giggle pulls pranks with glee,
Tickling the toes of a snoozing bee.
A gnome in the corner collects all the fuss,
As ivy and brambles form quite the ruckus.

A playful wind swirls with a wily grin,
Chasing the giggles, where's it been?
With leaves as umbrellas, they float and glide,
In this patch where humor takes its ride.

As evening cloaks these merry folks,
With firefly lanterns, they share their jokes.
For in this shade, with mirth and cheer,
Lies a secret of laughter that draws us near.

Constellations of the Canopy

Up high in branches, squirrels plot their schemes,
While robins join in with their chirpy dreams.
A raccoon juggles with some shiny charms,
As night returns, weaving jovial psalms.

The stars like glitter fall from a hat,
While wise old owls laugh, 'What's up with that?'
In shadows, the night creatures join the fun,
Chasing their tails, under moonlight spun.

A blanket of leaves becomes nature's stage,
Where critters perform without a wage.
As the crickets play tunes that tickle the air,
Each giggle and gleam shows they haven't a care.

The constellations dance overhead so bright,
In this playful spectacle, hearts take flight.
For in the trees, with whimsy's embrace,
Lies laughter that echoes, in a wild chase.

www.ingramcontent.com/pod-product-compliance
Lightning Source LLC
Chambersburg PA
CBHW051646160426
43209CB00004B/815